DEC 0 2 2009

W9-DJA-927

REMARKABLE PEOPLE

Miley Cyrus

by Jennifer Howse

DISCARD

MOORESVILLE PUBLIC LIBRARY
220 WEST HARRISON STREET
MOORESVILLE, INDIANA 46158

Published by Weigl Publishers Inc.
350 5th Avenue, Suite 3304, PMB 6G
New York, NY 10118-0069

Website: www.weigl.com

Copyright ©2009 WEIGL PUBLISHERS INC.
All rights reserved. No part of this publication may be reproduced, stored in a
retrieval system, or transmitted in any form or by any means, electronic, mechanical,
photocopying, recording, or otherwise, without the prior written permission of
the publisher.

All of the Internet URLs given in the book were valid at the time of publication.
However, due to the dynamic nature of the Internet, some addresses may have
changed, or sites may have ceased to exist since publication. While the author and
publisher regret any inconvenience this may cause readers, no responsibility for any
such changes can be accepted by either the author or the publisher.

Library of Congress Cataloging-in-Publication Data

Howse, Jennifer.
  Miley Cyrus / Jennifer Howse.
     p. cm. -- (Remarkable people)
  Includes index.
  ISBN 978-1-59036-984-5 (hard cover : alk. paper) -- ISBN 978-1-59036-985-2 (soft
cover : alk. paper)
  1. Cyrus, Miley, 1992---Juvenile literature. 2. Singers--United States--Biography--
Juvenile literature. 3. Actresses--United States--Biography--Juvenile literature. I.
Title.
  ML3930.C98H68 2009
  782.42164092--dc22
  [B]

                                   2008003965

Printed in the United States of America
 2 3 4 5 6 7 8 9 0 12 11 10 09

Editor: Danielle LeClair
Design: Terry Paulhus

Photograph Credits
Weigl acknowledges Getty Images as the primary image supplier for this title.
Unless otherwise noted, all images herein were obtained from Getty Images and
its contributors.

Other photograph credits include: **Alamy:** pages 3, 7 (background).

Every reasonable effort has been made to trace ownership and to obtain
permission to reprint copyright material. The publishers would be pleased
to have any errors or omissions brought to their attention so that they may
be corrected in subsequent printings.

Contents

Who Is Miley Cyrus?

Miley Cyrus is a singer, songwriter, actress, and teen sensation. She is best known to her fans as the star of the Disney television show *Hannah Montana*. On the show, Miley plays a girl who has a secret double life. At home and at school she is a typical girl, known as Miley Stewart. After school, she puts on a blond wig and becomes Hannah Montana, the biggest singing superstar on television. In real life, Miley is a teen pop star and a remarkable person. She has a successful television show, has sold out concerts, and has supported many charities. Miley has won fans around the world with her raspy singing voice and upbeat songs. She is a great **comedian** who knows how to make an audience laugh. Miley's smile, singing voice, outgoing personality, and hard work have made her one of the most popular teen stars today.

> *"You can live your dream, but never forget who your friends and family are."*

Growing Up

Destiny Hope Cyrus was born on November 23, 1992, in Franklin, Tennessee. Destiny's constant smile earned her the nickname "Smiley." Over time, Smiley was shortened to Miley. One of six children, Miley grew up on her parents' farm just outside of Nashville. Her parents are country singer and actor Billy Ray Cyrus and Leticia Cyrus. The year Miley was born, Billy Ray broke onto the country music scene with the hit song "Achy Breaky Heart." Billy Ray starred in the television series, *Doc*.

Growing up on a farm in Tennessee, Miley was surrounded by family, friends, and animals. She had a quiet life and attended Heritage Middle School until she got the role on *Hannah Montana*. Now, Miley travels around North America performing as Hannah Montana, as well as herself. Instead of going to a school, she has a private tutor who travels with her. Although Miley is away from home a great deal, she enjoys coming back to the farm. There, she has many pets, including horses, cats, fish, and chickens. Her three dogs are named Loco, Juicy, and Minnie Pearl.

■ Miley changed her name from Destiny Hope to Miley Ray. She chose Ray for her new middle name because she wanted to share a name with her dad.

Get to Know Tennessee

ANIMAL
Raccoon

FLAG

FLOWER
Iris

MISSOURI | KENTUCKY | VIRGINIA
TENNESSEE
NORTH CAROLINA
MISSISSIPPI | ALABAMA | GEORGIA | SOUTH CAROLINA

0   195 Miles
0   313 Kilometers

Singer and pop music superstar Justin Timberlake was born in Tennessee.

The Grand Ole Opry in Nashville, Tennessee, has been broadcasting its live radio program since 1925.

Bristol, Tennessee, is considered the birthplace of country music.

Tennesseean Alex Hailey won the **Nobel Prize** for his book *Roots*.

Nashville is called the country music capital of the world.

Think about it!

Music is a major industry in Tennessee. Miley is part of a large group of musicians who make the music industry important for the state. Make a chart of three different industries that are important in the region where you live. In each column, list at least three jobs that are available in these industries. Pick two jobs that interest you. What education do you need for these jobs? What are the job responsibilities?

Practice Makes Perfect

Miley plays the guitar and has a soulful singing voice. She enjoys writing music, playing the guitar, and singing old Elvis Presley songs. Playing an instrument is a skill that requires practice, and Miley tries to practice every day. She enjoys playing the guitar so much that she has taught her friend Emily Osment, an actor on *Hannah Montana*, how to play.

Songwriting is another skill that takes dedication to learn. Miley writes the lyrics to a song and then works with her dad on the music. Together, they have created many of the songs Miley sings and records. One song, which they perform together, is called "Ready, Set, Don't Go." It is about Miley's relationship with her father and how it is changing as she grows up.

■ Miley loves performing for an audience. She says there is nothing more fun than being on stage, and as soon as she starts singing, nothing else matters.

The first time Miley went on a concert tour, she was the opening act for the singing group The Cheetah Girls. Before going on tour with Miley, The Cheetah Girls starred in two popular television movies.

In October 2007, Miley launched the Best of Both Worlds Tour. The opening act was the Jonas Brothers. Playing for sold-out crowds, Miley works hard to prepare for each show. She spends long hours rehearsing with the band, as well as the stage and sound crews.

QUICK FACTS

- The album *Hannah Montana* was released in October 2006. Eight months later, *Hannah Montana II: Meet Miley Cyrus* was released.

- Miley co-wrote eight of the ten songs on her second album. They were credited to Destiny Hope Cyrus.

- Miley is a spokesperson for Daisy Guitars, which are a line of guitars for girls.

▪▪▪ In 2007, Miley and the Jonas Brothers performed together on "Dick Clark's New Year's Rockin' Eve" in New York's Times Square.

Key Events

Miley realized she wanted to become an actor when she was nine years old. She fell in love with acting after guest-starring on her father's television show, *Doc*. At the age of 11, Miley auditioned for the Disney show *Hannah Montana*. At first, she did not get the part. After practicing her singing and acting skills, Miley was given the role when she was 12.

In *Hannah Montana*, Miley's character faces the problems and difficulties of an average teenager, such as dealing with bullies or the demands of school. However, most of her friends do not know that Miley is the famous Hannah Montana. In each episode, Miley struggles to keep her rock star identity secret. Landing the lead role in *Hannah Montana* has sent Miley's career soaring.

The release of two albums *Hannah Montana* and *Hannah Montana II* have established Miley as a singer and songwriter. Her concert tours have given her a chance to perform as the character Hannah Montana, but also as herself, Miley Cyrus. Fans are now getting to know the real Miley.

■ Miley named the character she plays. Disney Channel was going to call the show *Alexis Texas*. Miley suggested *Hannah Montana,* and the show's producers loved it.

Thoughts from Miley

Miley loves to perform as much as she loves her friends and family. Here are some of her thoughts about life as a teen star.

Miley tries to decide what she loves more, singing or acting.

"It depends because acting is so cool, like being on set and that kind of thing. But singing is a better way to be yourself, so I can't choose."

Miley takes her father's advice.

"He takes everything one step at a time and it's kind of what he's taught me to do."

Miley talks about growing up.

"You don't have to fall into what everyone else is doing. I try my hardest just to stay grounded, because I have all these different kinds of people that are older than me, trying to tell me what to do. I just have to say be true to yourself. Be a kid. Grow up slowly."

Miley has always loved singing.

"My dad says I could sing before I could talk, if that's possible. I was always humming and things like that."

Miley talks about being recognized.

"I don't get annoyed when fans come up to me, but sometimes I get nervous. It's like what am I gonna do, what am I supposed to say, do I look the way they would want me to?"

Miley enjoys being on stage.

"I feel very nervous. I get really kinda scared right before I go on. But once you're out there you forget everything."

What Is a Singer?

Singing is something most people do. A professional singer is someone who works hard to perfect the sound of his or her voice, and gets paid to sing for others. Miley has never taken formal singing lessons. She grew up listening to her father sing, and singing with him when he was home. Singing is a skill that requires practice and patience to get a song just right.

Miley's favorite singers are Kelly Clarkson and Mariah Carey. Both of these women have a wide vocal range. This means they can reach very high notes and very low notes with their voices. Miley reads music. This is another important skill for a singer. It helps a singer to understand how loud and in what **pitch** and **key** a song should be sung. Miley's favorite song to perform is "Nobody's Perfect."

■ Kelly Clarkson was the first winner of American Idol. Like Miley, she has never had singing lessons.

Singers 101

Avril Lavigne (1984–)

Achievements: Singer, songwriter, actress, and model
Born in Napanee, Ontario, Canada, Avril understands the pressures of stardom at a young age. In 2002, when Avril was 18 years old, she released the CD *Let Go*. She was nominated for eight **Grammy awards,** including New Artist of the Year and Album of the Year. 16 million copies were sold worldwide. Avril also acts and models, but she is still first and foremost a singer.

LeAnne Rimes (1982–)

Achievements: Singer
At the age of 13, country singer LeAnne recorded "Blue." It became an instant hit. LeAnne is known for having a powerful voice, as well as for being a great songwriter. By the age of 24, LeAnne had sold more than 37 million copies of her albums. She is the youngest person to win a Grammy award. LeAnne has also won American Music awards and Billboard Music awards.

Hillary Duff (1987–)

Achievements: Singer and actress
A singer and actor, Hillary's first major role was in *Casper Meets Wendy*. She was then cast in the hit television series *Lizzie McGuire*. This series became a full-length feature film in 2003. In addition to acting, Hillary has recorded two albums. *Metamorphosis* sold more than two million copies. Between touring with her band and acting in movies, Hillary supports many charities, including shelters for homeless people. She also has a line of clothing for girls and teens.

Selena Perez (1971–1995)

Achievements: Singer
By the age of nine, Selena was performing with her parents and brothers and sisters. Singing the **tejano** style of music, Selena was well-known in the Latin community for her powerful voice and lively dance moves. Selena was a role model. She enjoyed spending time with family and was active in anti-drug campaigns and AIDS awareness programs. At the age of 24, Selina died, but her legacy continues with her fans. An album released after her death, called "Dreaming of You," was the first tejano album to reach number one on the U.S. music charts.

Guitar

A guitar is a musical instrument that is played by plucking or strumming the strings. The long neck of a guitar is separated by a metal strips, or frets. While one hand strums the guitar, the other hand presses the strings along the frets. The main body of the guitar is flat-backed or rounded to create a rich sound. Guitars have four main types: acoustic, electric, classical, and Spanish. Traditionally made from rosewood, guitars are also made from maple or mahogany.

Influences

Miley's greatest influence and best friend is her dad, Billy Ray Cyrus. Miley admires her father's success as an actor and country singer. She trusts his musical guidance. The first time Miley sang in front of an audience was with her dad. They sang Elvis Presley's "Hound Dog" at one of Billy Ray's concerts. Billy Ray has said, "Miley's got a great heart. She's got a great head on her shoulders."

Throughout her rise to stardom, Billy Ray has supported Miley's dreams to act and perform. He has made sure that Miley knows her family is behind her in good times and in bad. The pressure to perform is very hard on young stars like Miley. Billy Ray has helped Miley to stay grounded. This means she must do the same things as other kids, including chores and attending church on Sunday with her family.

◼ In 2008, Miley and her dad hosted the Country Music Television Music awards.

Miley was able to work with Dolly Parton on the *Hannah Montana* show. Dolly is a country singer, songwriter, and actor, who is from Miley's home state of Tennessee. Dolly played the part of Hannah's godmother on the show. Her character offers advice and helps Hannah out of some difficulties. Like the character on the show, Dolly is proud to be an influence in Miley's life. She believes Miley is a great singer, actress, and comedian. Dolly thinks Miley is going to be a huge star.

THE CYRUS FAMILY

The Cyrus family includes Billy Ray and Miley's mother Leticia, or Tish. Miley has five brothers and sisters. Her two older half-brothers are Christopher Cody and Trace. Her older half-sister is Brandi. The younger siblings are her brother Braison and sister Noah Lindsey. Christopher Cody is a vocalist and guitarist for the rock band Metro Station. Noah Lindsey also loves to act and has appeared in an episode of *Hannah Montana* as a guest star.

■■ Miley's family loves to spend time together. They enjoy playing ping pong and shooting pool.

MOORESVILLE PUBLIC LIBRARY
220 WEST HARRISON STREET
MOORESVILLE, INDIANA 46158

Overcoming Obstacles

iley thinks concert tours, public appearances, and working on a television show are all very exciting. On each of these projects, she works very hard, and at times, for long hours. Miley tries to give excellent performances. She always wants to be her best in every concert, public appearance, and *Hannah Montana* episode. This is a great deal of pressure for a person to be under.

■ Miley loves being with her fans. She says that, when little girls asks for her autograph, she realizes how lucky she is to be living out her dream.

At times, Miley says she would like to rest and just spend time with her family and friends. Being away from her family is a challenge, so Miley's mother makes sure that holidays and Sundays are family times.

Another difficulty for Miley is that sometimes people say or write things about her that are not true. In 2007, a person posted a false story about her on the Internet. Miley's feelings were hurt by the **rumor**. To help her overcome these challenges, Miley goes to her father for advice. He has always told her, "you can't live a positive life with a negative mind, so always be positive."

■ Fans, young and old, love Miley. In all 22 cities that the Best of Both Worlds tour visited, tickets for the concert tour sold out within minutes.

Achievements and Successes

In 2003, Miley had her first role in a movie. She played young Ruthie in the movie *Big Fish*. Miley auditioned for her role on *Hannah Montana* more than 10 times. At first, she tried out for the part of Hannah's best friend, but the people at Disney thought she was too small and too young. This was difficult for Miley, but the producers told her how she could improve her skills as an actor. Miley kept trying. She continued to audition for *Hannah Montana* until she won the part. Miley's **persistence** has paid off with a number-one rated television series and sold-out concert tours.

Miley has won many awards, including the 2007 Teen Choice award for TV Actress in a Comedy and for Breakout Star.

■ At the 2007 Teen Choice awards, one of the awards Miley won was Choice Summer Artist.

Miley's first movie was *Hannah Montana/Miley Cyrus Best of Both Worlds Concert Tour*. This 3-D film of her concert tour includes on-stage performances and behind-the-scenes action. In 2008, the Disney company asked Miley to write a book. They wanted Miley to tell the story of her early life in Tennessee, her role on Hannah Montana, and her close relationship with her parents. The book, as well as her concerts, movies, and television show, have made Miley one of the highest-paid teenagers in the world.

Miley's concerts are popular with children and teens. She uses this success to help others. From the Best of Both Worlds tour, one dollar from each ticket sold was donated to the City of Hope Cancer Research and Treatment Center.

CITY OF HOPE

The City of Hope helps people who have cancer, diabetes, and other life-threatening illnesses. Located in Duarte, California, this hospital is ranked as one of the best cancer hospitals in the United States. Miley believes that cancer is devastating, especially when it impacts children and teens. The money raised from concert sales helps children being treated at the hospital. Miley feels fortunate to be able to help support the City of Hope. For more information about the center, check its website at **www.cityofhope.org**.

Write a Biography

A person's life story can be the subject of a book. This kind of book is called a biography. Biographies describe the lives of remarkable people, such as those who have achieved great success or have done important things to help others. These people may be alive today, or they may have lived many years ago. Reading a biography can help you learn more about a remarkable person.

At school, you might be asked to write a biography. First, decide who you want to write about. You can choose a singer, such as Miley Cyrus, or any other person you find interesting. Then, find out if your library has any books about this person. Learn as much as you can about him or her. Write down the key events in this person's life. What was this person's childhood like? What has he or she accomplished? What are his or her goals? What makes this person special or unusual?

A concept web is a useful research tool. Read the questions in the following concept web. Answer the questions in your notebook. Your answers will help you write your biography review.

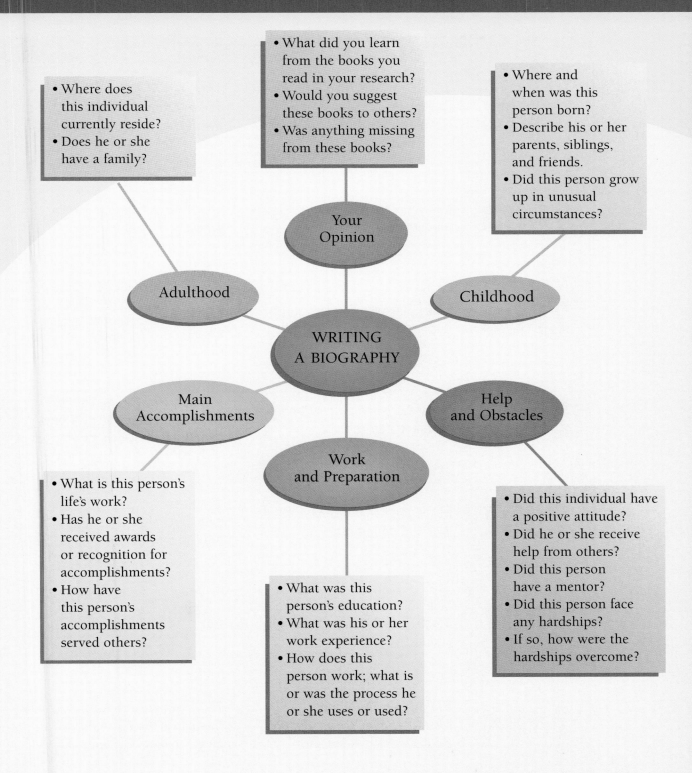

- Where does this individual currently reside?
- Does he or she have a family?

- What did you learn from the books you read in your research?
- Would you suggest these books to others?
- Was anything missing from these books?

- Where and when was this person born?
- Describe his or her parents, siblings, and friends.
- Did this person grow up in unusual circumstances?

Your Opinion

Adulthood

Childhood

WRITING A BIOGRAPHY

Main Accomplishments

Help and Obstacles

Work and Preparation

- What is this person's life's work?
- Has he or she received awards or recognition for accomplishments?
- How have this person's accomplishments served others?

- What was this person's education?
- What was his or her work experience?
- How does this person work; what is or was the process he or she uses or used?

- Did this individual have a positive attitude?
- Did he or she receive help from others?
- Did this person have a mentor?
- Did this person face any hardships?
- If so, how were the hardships overcome?

Timeline

YEAR	MILEY CYRUS	WORLD EVENTS
1992	Destiny Hope Cyrus is born on November 23.	The Internet is made available to the public for the first time.
2003	Miley has her first acting role on the TV show *Doc*.	The Disney Pixar film *Finding Nemo* is released.
2003	Miley plays the role of young Ruthie in the movie *Big Fish*.	*Harry Potter and the Order of the Phoenix*, a book by J.K. Rowling, is published.
2006	Miley stars in the first *Hannah Montana* episode.	MTV awards *Pirates of the Caribbean: Dead Man's Chest* with the Best Movie of the Year.
2007	Miley goes on the Best of Both Worlds Concert tour.	Singer Carrie Underwood wins Best New Artist at the Grammy awards.
2007	Miley is chosen as one of *People Magazine's* 100 most beautiful people in the world.	Actor Heath Ledger dies.
2008	The 3-D movie *Hannah Montana/Miley Cyrus: Best of Both Worlds* is released.	The *Chronicles of Narnia: Prince Caspian* is the second Narnia movie to open in theaters.

Further Research

How can I find out more about Miley Cyrus?

Most libraries have computers that connect to a database that contains information on books and articles about different subjects. You can input a key word and find material on the person, place, or thing you want to learn more about. The computer will provide you with a list of books in the library that contain information on the subject you searched for. Non-fiction books are arranged numerically, using their call number. Fiction books are organized alphabetically by the author's last name.

Websites

Find out more about Miley Cyrus, at
www.mileyworld.com

To learn more about *Hannah Montana*, visit
http://home.disney.go.com/tv/index

Words to Know

comedian: a person who entertains by telling jokes and acting in a way that makes people laugh

Grammy awards: an award given to musicians for outstanding work

key: the main tone of the scale in a musical work

Nobel Prize: an international prize to recognize the person, people, or groups who make an important impact in their field

persistence: being steadfast, determined, stubborn, or insistent

pitch: the high or low quality of a sound or musical note

rumor: a piece of information shared between people without any proof that it is true

tejano: a style of music that is based on Latin rhythm

Index